SRA Reading Mastery

Signature Edition

Workbook B

Siegfried Engelmann
Susan Hanner

SRA

A Division of The McGraw-Hill Companies
Columbus, OH

Illustration Credits
Rick Cooley, Heidi King, Simon Galkin,
Dan Schofield, Jim Shough, and Jessica Stanley

READING MASTERY® is a registered trademark of The McGraw-Hill Companies, Inc.

SRAonline.com

 SRA

A Division of The McGraw-Hill Companies

Send all inquiries to this address:
SRA/McGraw-Hill
4400 Easton Commons
Columbus, OH 43219

ISBN: 978-0-07-612546-3
MHID: 0-07-612546-7

14 HES 13

Name _____

A

1. Jean is 2 miles high. Fran is 5 miles high. Who is colder? _____

2. Tell why.
   • because she is colder
   • because she is higher
   • because she is lower

B Story Items

3. How far is the trip from Japan to Italy?
   • 6 hundred miles   • 6 thousand miles
                • 60 thousand miles

4. How long should that trip take?
   • 6 hours   • 12 hours   • 13 hours

5. **Underline** 2 countries the plane flew over on the trip.
   • Turkey   • United States   • Canada
        • England   • China

6. **Underline** the state in the United States that is bigger than Italy.
   • Ohio   • Alaska   • New York

7. Italy is shaped something like a ▮▮▮.
        • horn   • shoe   • boot

8. When could Herman move fastest?

- when it is 60 degrees
- when it is 50 degrees
- when it is 80 degrees
- when it is 45 degrees

9. Write **north, south, east,** and **west** in the right boxes.
10. Make a **J** where Japan is.
11. Make a **C** where China is.
12. Make a **T** where Turkey is.
13. Make an **I** where Italy is.
14. Is the United States shown on this map? _____

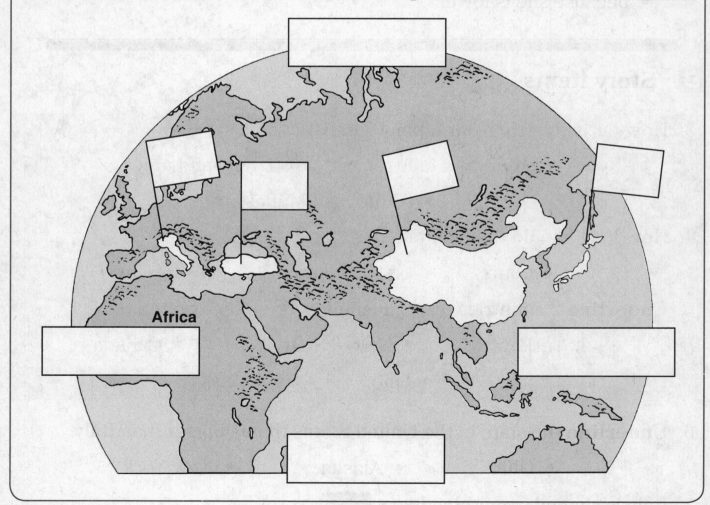

Africa

GO TO PART D IN YOUR TEXTBOOK.

Name _____

Story Items

> 1. **Circle** 2 of the things below that would smell very good to Herman.
>
> 2. **Underline** one thing that would smell bad to Herman.
>
> - meat   • soap   • candy   • garbage   • gum

3. A plane that flies from Italy to New York City goes in

   which direction? _____

4. What airport did Herman fly to in this story?

   - San Francisco   • Kennedy   • Italy

5. In what city is that airport?

   - Chicago   • San Francisco   • New York City

6. Where are the fuel tanks on a big jet?

   - in the rear   • in the wings   • in the galley

7. It was hard for Herman to move around in the fall

   because ▮▮▮.

   - it was raining   • the temperature went up
   - the temperature went down

8. What killed Herman?

   - freezing   • boiling   • sleeping

9. Which letter shows where Italy is? _____

10. Which letter shows where New York City is? _____

11. Which letter shows where Turkey is? _____

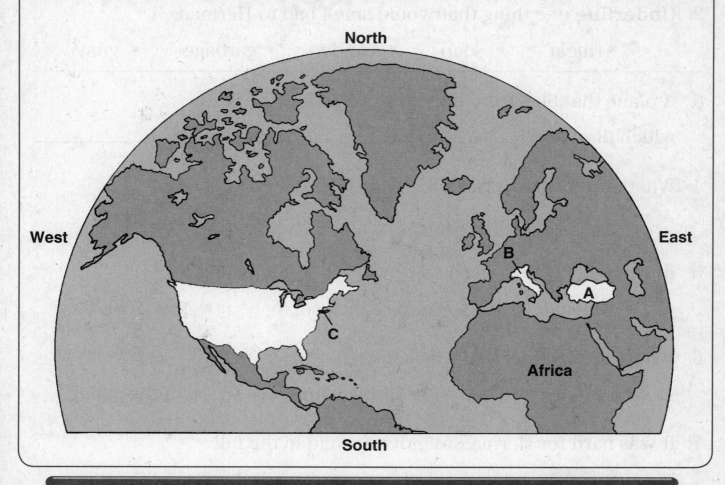

Review Items

12. Sue is 10 miles high. Lynn is 6 miles high. Who is

    colder? _____

13. Tell why. _____

GO TO PART C IN YOUR TEXTBOOK.

Name _____

A

The picture shows 4 objects caught in a whirlpool.

1. Write **1** on the object that will go down the hole in the whirlpool first.

2. Write **2** on the object that will go down next.

3. Number the rest of the objects.

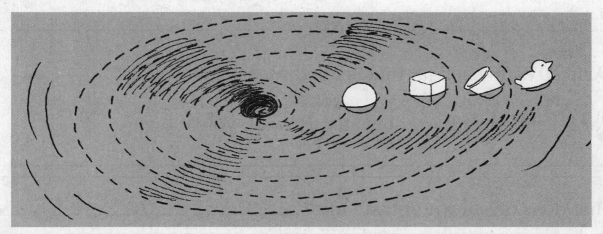

B

4. Put a **B** on 2 bulkheads.

5. Put an **X** on 2 decks.

6. Put a **W** at the bow.

7. Put an **S** at the stern.

C

The picture below shows jars of water on a very cold day.

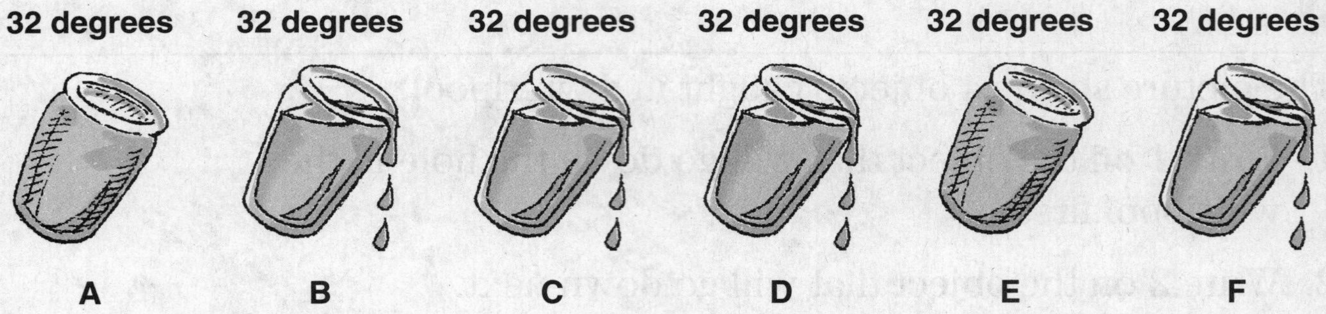

32 degrees	32 degrees	32 degrees	32 degrees	32 degrees	32 degrees
A	B	C	D	E	F

8. What is the temperature of the water in each jar?

_____

9. Write **OW** on each jar that is filled with ocean water.

10. Jar F is filled with ocean water. How do you know?

_____

11. What does ocean water taste like? _____

12. What will happen if you drink a lot of ocean water?

_____

GO TO PART F IN YOUR TEXTBOOK.

Name _____

Story Items

1. Linda and Kathy were on a ship that was going from the United States to ▮▮▮▮.

    • Canada   • England   • Japan

2. The girls were on their way to visit their _____.

3. Did Linda and Kathy go in one of the lifeboats when the ship sank?

    _____

4. What did the girls plan to use for a lifeboat?

    • a raft   • a crate   • a boat

5. Which girl could swim well?

    • Linda   • Kathy

6. Which girl was older? _____

7. How much older? _____

8. When the ship sank, it was in the middle of the _____ Ocean.

9. A stranger lifted ▮▮▮▮ into a lifeboat.

    • Linda   • Kathy

10. Why didn't she stay in the lifeboat?

    • She went to find her sister.   • She was scared.

    • She couldn't swim.

Review Items

11. Write **north, south, east,** and **west** in the right boxes.

12. Which letter shows where Japan is? _____

13. Which letter shows where Italy is? _____

14. Which letter shows where Turkey is? _____

15. Which letter shows where China is? _____

16. Is the United States shown on this map? _____

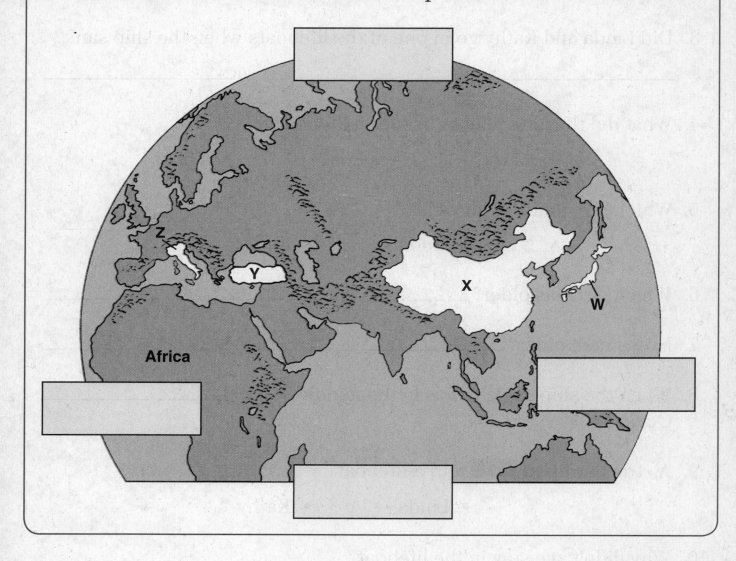

GO TO PART C IN YOUR TEXTBOOK.

Story Items

1. Why did Linda have a hard time swimming to the crate?

    • She could not swim well.   • Currents held her back.

                        • She was weak.

2. What did Linda and Kathy use for a lifeboat?

                • a raft   • a craft   • a crate

3. What did the girls use for paddles?   • oars   • hands   • boards

4. What made Linda's feet sore?

        • the crate   • the salt water   • the sun

5. If you drank lots of ocean water, you would get ▮▮▮▮.

            • sillier   • tired   • thirstier

Here's a picture of Kathy and Linda on their crate.

6. Which arrow shows the way Linda's hand will move? _____

7. Which arrow shows the way the crate will move? _____

---

8. Something made sounds that told Linda they were near the shore. What made those sounds?

    • waves on the beach   • birds in the trees   • fish in the waves

9. As the girls walked along the beach, they could hardly see where they

    were going. Tell why. _____

Review Items

10. Write **north, south, east,** and **west** in the right boxes.

11. Which letter shows where China is? _____

12. Which letter shows where Japan is? _____

13. Is the United States shown on this map? _____

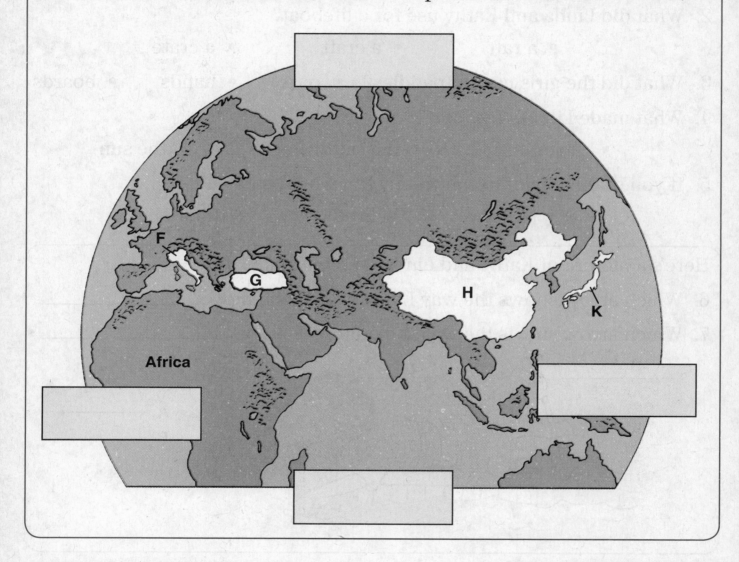

GO TO PART D IN YOUR TEXTBOOK.

Name _____

1. Palm trees cannot live in places that get ▉▉▉▉.
   - wet   - cold   - moist

2. What are the branches of palm trees called?
   - fans   - fonds   - fronds

3. When the author told about palm trees, was the purpose to **persuade,**
   inform, or **entertain?** _____

B Story Items

4. Underline 2 words that tell about the stream water.
   - cold   - warm   - salty   - smelly   - dark   - fresh

5. A strange sound woke Linda in the morning. What was making that
   strange sound?
   - sailors   - birds   - waves

6. Whose footprints did Linda and Kathy find on the beach?

   _____

7. Linda said, "We have been walking in a circle. That means
   we're ▉▉▉▉."
   - in a forest   - near Japan   - on an island

8. Did Linda and Kathy see anyone else when they were

   walking? _____

9. When the author told about Linda and Kathy, was the purpose to
   persuade, inform, or **entertain?** _____

The map shows the island that Linda and Kathy were on.

10. Write **north, south, east,** and **west** in the right boxes.

11. **Draw a line** from the crate to show where Linda and Kathy walked.

12. **Make an X** to show where Linda was when she saw footprints.

13. **Make a Y** to show where they landed on the island.

14. **Make an S** to show where the stream is.

15. **Circle** the grove where they found bananas.

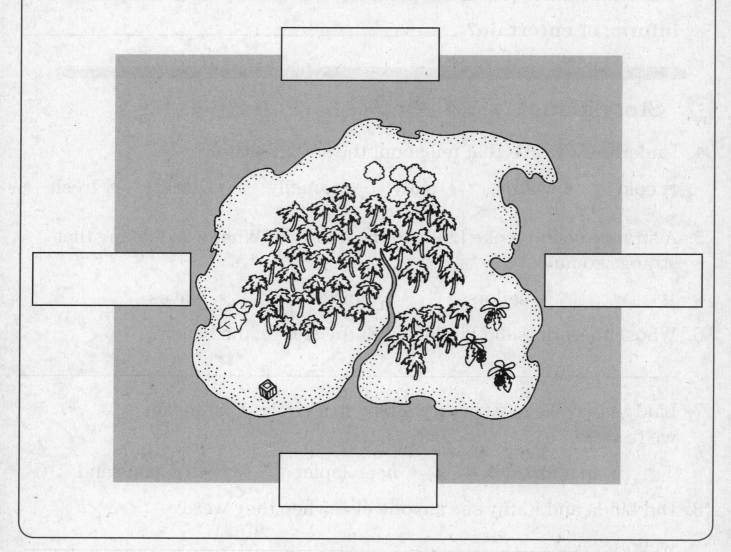

GO TO PART D IN YOUR TEXTBOOK.

Name _____

Story Items

1. What was wrong with the first coconuts that the girls found?

   - They were too high in the trees.

   - They were not ripe.

   - They were rotten.

2. When Kathy shook the coconut, it sounded like a bottle that had water in it. What made the sound like water?

   _____

3. What did Linda and Kathy use to open the coconut?

   _____

4. Why did the girls want to make the monkeys mad?

   - so they would throw coconuts

   - so they would go away

   - so they would make noise

The picture shows a coconut.

5. Make an **X** on the part that the girls ate.

6. Make a **Y** on the part that the girls drank.

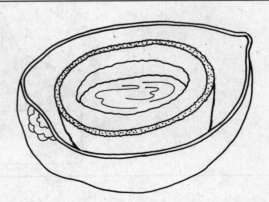

Review Items

The map shows the island that Linda and Kathy were on.

7. Write **north, south, east,** and **west** in the right boxes.

8. **Draw a line** from the crate to show where Linda and Kathy walked.

9. **Make an A** to show where Linda was when she saw footprints.

10. **Make a B** to show where they landed on the island.

11. **Make a C** to show where the stream is.

12. **Circle** the grove where they found bananas.

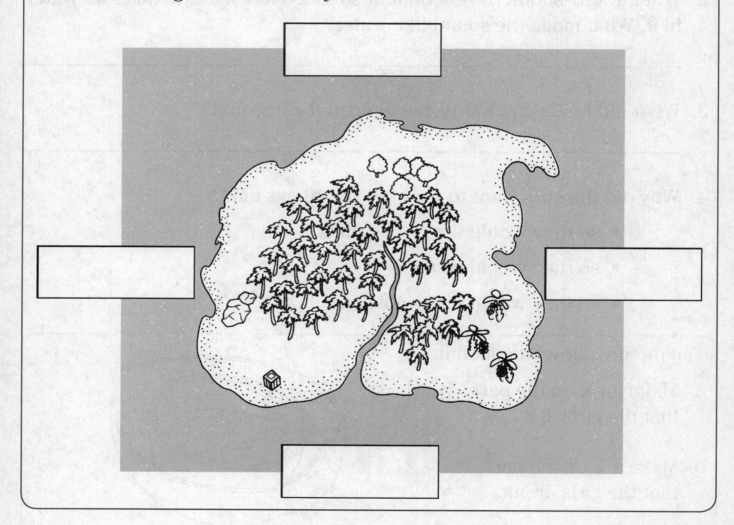

GO TO PART D IN YOUR TEXTBOOK.

Name _____

A

1. All machines make it easier for someone to _____.

2. You would have the most power if you pushed against handle C.

    Which handle would give you the least amount of power?

    _____

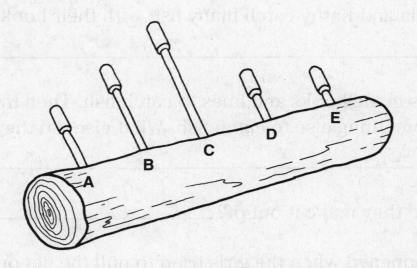

B **Story Items**

3. What were the only things Linda and Kathy ate for two days?

    - carrots
    - coconuts
    - corn
    - fronds
    - cabbage
    - bananas

Lesson 58   **15**

4. Why did Linda and Kathy want to catch some fish?

- They were tired.

- They wanted to eat something new.

- They could not open the coconuts.

5. What did they use for fish hooks? _____

6. What did they use for a fishing line? _____

7. Were there many fish in the water? _____

8. Did Linda and Kathy catch many fish with their hooks and

   lines? _____

9. The girls made hooks and lines to catch fish. Then they made something else to catch fish. What else did they

   make? _____

10. What did they make it out of? _____

11. What happened when the girls tried to pull the net out of the water?

- The fish jumped out of the water.

- The fish pulled the girls into the water.

- The crate fell in the water.

GO TO PART D IN YOUR TEXTBOOK.

Name _____

Story Items

1. Linda and Kathy built something to help them ▮▮▮▮.
    - pull the nails from the crate
    - pull the net from the ocean
    - pull Kathy's teeth

2. What did the girls find floating in the water?
    - a ship
    - a first-aid kit
    - boards

3. The white box probably came from ▮▮▮▮.
    - their ship
    - their crate
    - Italy

4. What was the most important thing inside the box?
    - candy
    - food
    - matches

5. Why didn't the girls test them right away?
    - They would need them later.
    - They didn't know how.
    - They were tired.

6. The girls made a ▮▮▮▮.
    - building
    - machine
    - motor

7. What did the girls use for a handle?
    - a board
    - a log
    - a vine

8. The girls hammered the handle to the end of ▮▮▮▮.

  • a shoe   • a log   • a crate

9. The girls got nails from ▮▮▮▮.

  • a shoe   • a log   • a crate

10. They tied one end of the vine to the log and the other end of the vine to the ▮▮▮▮.

  • beach   • crate   • net

11. When the fish were in the net, the girls ▮▮▮▮.

  • turned the handle   • ran into the water

  • climbed a tree

12. The arrow by the handle shows which way it turns. Start at the dot on the log. Make an arrow on the log to show which way it turns.

13. Make an arrow by the vine to show which way it moves.

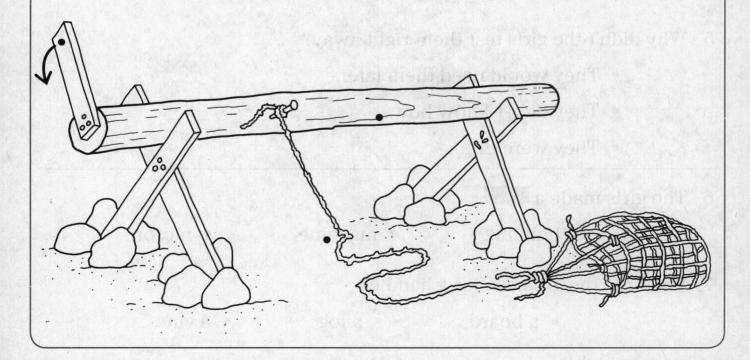

GO TO PART C IN YOUR TEXTBOOK.

Name _____

A

1. What is it called when the sun goes down?

   • sunrise   • sunset

2. What is it called when the sun comes up?

   • sunrise   • sunset

B **Story Items**

3. What did Kathy have to do to the outside of the fish?

   • remove fins   • remove scales   • remove shells

4. What did she use for a tool?

   • a fin   • a scale   • a shell

5. What was Linda's job when the girls cleaned the fish?

   • removing the scales   • removing the insides

   • removing the fins

6. What did she use for a tool?

   • a belt buckle   • a nail   • a rock

7. Linda made her tool sharp by ▓▓▓▓.

   • rubbing it against a rock   • putting it in the fire

   • making it red hot

8. Name 2 things the girls ate for dinner.

   1 _____

   2 _____

9. Linda and Kathy drank fresh water with their dinner.

   Where did they get the fresh water? _____

10. **Underline** 4 things that the girls used to make their simple machine.

   - vines
   - boards
   - turtle shell

   - nails
   - rope
   - matches

   - coconuts
   - a tree trunk

Review Items

11. The arrow by the handle shows which way it turns. Make an arrow on the log to show which way it moves.

12. Make an arrow by the vine to show which way it moves.

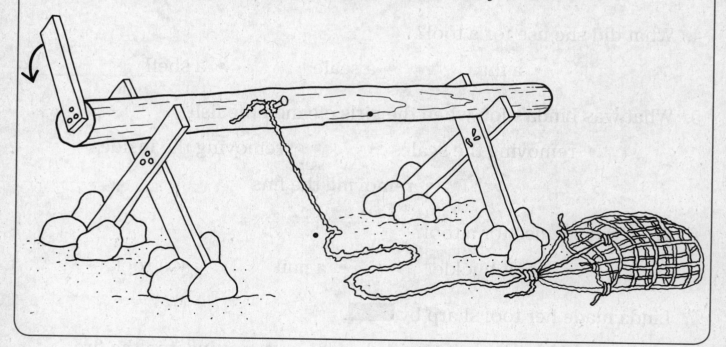

GO TO PART D IN YOUR TEXTBOOK.

Name _____

Ⓐ

1. The temperature inside your body is about _____ degrees.

2. Most fevers don't go over _____ degrees.

3. When people have very high fevers, they may see and hear things that are not _____.

Ⓑ Story Items

4. How long had Linda and Kathy been on the island when they saw the airplane?

   • 15 days   • 3 weeks   • 12 days

5. Did the people in the plane see Linda and Kathy? _____

6. What did the girls use to make a signal for planes?

   • paint   • rocks   • leaves

7. What word did they spell? _____

8. The word was more than _____ feet long.

9. What kind of signal did the girls have ready for ships?

   • rocks   • fog   • smoke

10. What would make the fire smoke?

   • sticks   • green leaves   • bananas

Lesson 62   **21**

11. How did Linda know that Kathy had a fever?

  - Linda felt her forehead.

  - Linda took her temperature.

  - Linda felt her feet.

12. Linda thought that Kathy's temperature was over

  _____ degrees.

Review Items

13. The United States is a _____.

  - city   - state   - country

14. Japan is a _____.

15. How many states are in the United States? _____

GO TO PART D IN YOUR TEXTBOOK.

Name _____

A

63

1. Put a **T** on each tugboat.

2. Put a **D** on each dock.

3. Put an **S** on each ship.

B Story Items

4. How long had Linda and Kathy been on the island when they saw the airplane?

   • 15 days   • 3 weeks   • 12 days

5. Did the people in the plane see Linda and Kathy? _____

6. What did the girls use to make a signal for planes?

   • paint   • rocks   • leaves

7. What word did they spell? _____

8. The word was over _____ feet long.

9. What kind of signal did the girls have ready for ships?

  • rocks   • fog   • smoke

10. What made the fire smoke so much?

  • sticks   • green leaves   • bananas

11. What was the name of the ship that rescued the girls?

  • S. S. Mason   • S. S. Milton   • S. S. Sisters

12. Kathy's forehead was hot because she had a _____.

13. How long were the girls on the island?

  • one week   • 2 weeks   • almost 3 weeks

14. How long were the girls on the S.S. Milton?

  • one week   • 2 weeks   • almost 3 weeks

15. Where did the S.S. Milton take them? _____

16. Who took them to their new home? _____

17. Did Linda think it would be dull there? _____

18. Linda showed Captain Reeves 4 things that she and Kathy had used to survive on the island. **Underline** those 4 things.

  • machine   • belt buckle   • table   • books
  • TV   • wagon   • house   • socks
  • bathtub   • fish net   • vines

Review Items

19. The temperature inside your body is about _____ degrees when your body is healthy.

20. Most fevers don't go over _____ degrees.

GO TO PART D IN YOUR TEXTBOOK.

Name _____

A

1. Make a **K** on the map where Troy used to be.

2. Make a **P** where Greece is.

3. Make an **X** on Italy.

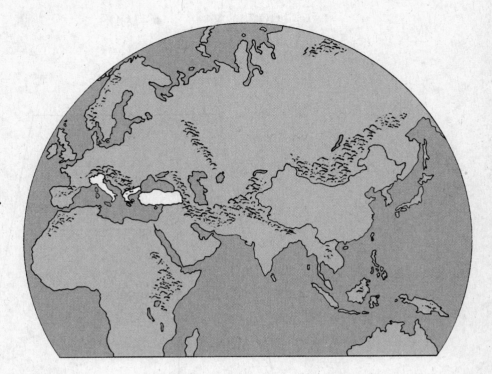

4. The place that was called Troy is now part of what country?

- Italy   • Greece   • Turkey

B **Story Items**

5. What year is it now? _____

6. In what year were you born? _____

7. In what year was the first airplane made? _____

8. What was the year 1 hundred years ago? _____

9. What was the year 2 hundred years ago? _____

10. In what year did the United States become a country? _____

11. What was the year 3 hundred years ago? _____

12. Write the years where they belong on the time line.

- 1995
- 1994
- 1997
- 1998
- 1990

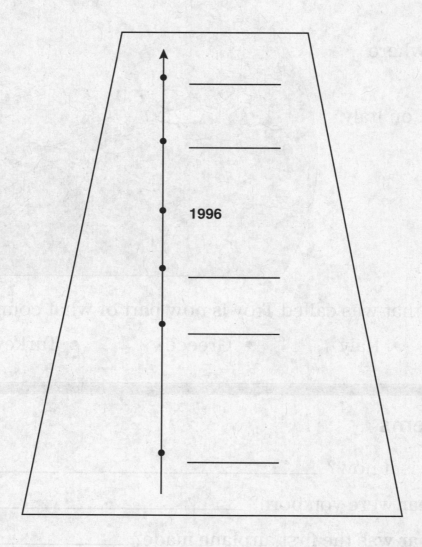

1996

GO TO PART D IN YOUR TEXTBOOK.

Name _____

Story Items

1. When did the story of Troy take place?

    • 300 years ago   • 3 thousand years ago

          • 1 thousand years ago

2. Why didn't the people of Troy have cars?

    • They didn't like cars.   • There were no cars yet.

          • Cars cost too much.

3. The people of Troy got in and out of the city through the great

    _____.

4. **Underline** the weapons that soldiers used when they had battles with Troy.

    • swords   • guns   • spears   • tanks

    • planes   • rockets   • bows   • arrows

5. When an army put ladders against the wall of Troy, what did the people of Troy do to the ladders?

    _____

6. When an army dug holes under the wall, what did the people of Troy dump into the holes? _____

7. When an army tried to knock down the gate, what did the people of Troy dump on them? _____

8. An army could not starve the people of Troy because the people had

    _____.

9. Write the years where they belong on the timeline.

- 1985   - 1982   - 1987   - 1981   - 1989

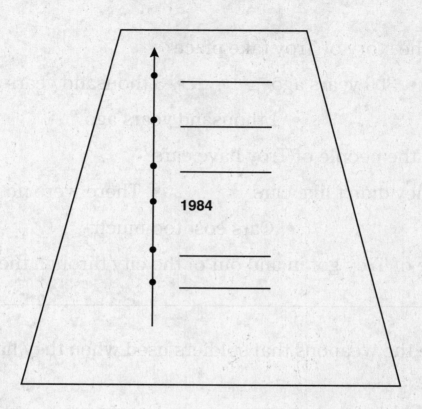

1984

GO TO PART C IN YOUR TEXTBOOK.

Name _____

A

Fill in the blanks on the time line.

1. Write **NOW** next to the dot that shows the year now.

2. Write **3 thousand years ago** next to the right dot.

3. Write **2 thousand years ago** next to the right dot.

4. Write **1 hundred years ago** next to the right dot.

5. Write **1 thousand years ago** next to the right dot.

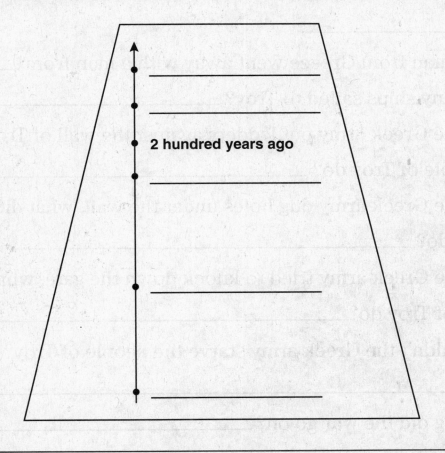

2 hundred years ago

6. How long ago did the story of Troy take place?

_____

7. About how long ago did Jesus Christ live?

_____

B **Story Items**

8. Greece went to war with Troy because of a woman named

_____.

9. The woman from Greece was important because she was a

_____.

10. The woman from Greece went away with a man from _____.

11. How many ships sailed to Troy? _____

12. When the Greek army put ladders against the wall of Troy, what did
the people of Troy do? _____

13. When the Greek army dug holes under the wall, what did the people
of Troy do? _____

14. When the Greek army tried to knock down the gate, what did the
people of Troy do?_____

15. Why couldn't the Greek army starve the people of Troy?

_____

16. How long did the war go on? _____

17. If the Greek army got a few men inside the wall of Troy, these men
could _____.

GO TO PART D IN YOUR TEXTBOOK.

Story Items

The army of Greece kept using the same four plans.

1. The army put ladders against _____.

2. The army dug holes _____.

3. The army tried to knock down _____.

4. The army kept the people of Troy _____.

5. How long did the war between Greece and Troy go on?

    _____

6. What did the Greek army build to help them get inside Troy?

    _____

7. Where did the army put the horse after they finished building it?

    _____

8. What did the people of Troy think the wooden horse was?

    • a cow   • a trick   • a gift

9. After the people of Troy fell asleep, what came out of the horse?

    _____

10. What did they do after they came out of the horse?

    _____

11. Was the great wooden horse a gift, or was it a trick?

    _____

12. Who won the war, Troy or Greece? _____

Review Items

Fill in the blanks on the time line.

13. Write **now** next to the dot that shows the year now.

14. Write **1 thousand years ago** next to the right dot.

15. Write **3 thousand years ago** next to the right dot.

16. Write **2 hundred years ago** next to the right dot.

17. Write **2 thousand years ago** next to the right dot.

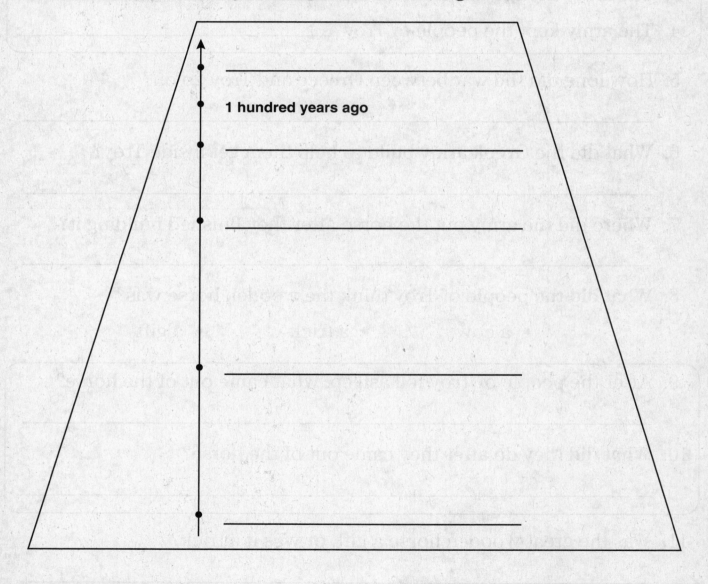

1 hundred years ago

GO TO PART C IN YOUR TEXTBOOK.

Name _____

A Story Items

1. How old was Bertha? _____

2. What kind of school did Bertha go to? _____

3. Bertha had a super sense of _____.

4. Who had a better sense of smell, Bertha or a hound dog?

   _____

5. Bertha and her friends played Pin the Tail on the Donkey. Did any of

   Bertha's friends pin the tail in the right place? _____

6. Did Bertha pin the tail in the right place? _____

7. Bertha knew what her friends at the party were doing without looking

   at them. How did she know? _____

8. **Underline** 2 things that were in the cans that the school tester used
   to test Bertha's sense of smell.

   • pepper   • roses   • oranges   • lilies   • lemon

9. Bertha was sorry that she had let people know about her sense of

   smell because she didn't want to be ███.

   • the same as others   • different from others   • others

B Skill Items

10. Compare Bertha and a hound dog. Remember, first tell how they're
    the same. Then tell how they're different.

    _____

    _____

    _____

Review Items

Write **W** for warm-blooded animals and **C** for cold-blooded animals.

11. beetle _____

12. cow _____

13. horse _____

14. spider _____

15. bee _____

The ship in the picture is sinking. It is making currents as it sinks.

16. Write the letter of the object that will go down the whirlpool first. _____

17. Write the letter of the object that will go down the whirlpool next. _____

18. Write the letter of the object that will go down the whirlpool last. _____

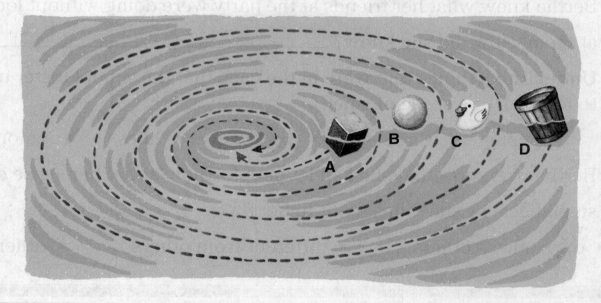

19. The temperature inside your body is about _____ degrees when you are healthy.

20. Most fevers don't go over _____ degrees.

GO TO PART C IN YOUR TEXTBOOK.

A Story Items

1. Bertha became restless after school got out for the summer. Tell why.

   • She didn't have anything to do.   • She didn't have a car.

          • She had a fight with her neighbors.

2. What is Maria Sanchez's job?

          • investor   • investigator   • illustrator

3. Had Maria finished her report? _____

4. Where was the oil company supposed to get its water?

          • from deep wells   • from the creek

5. Where did Maria think the oil company was getting its water?

          • from deep wells   • from the creek

6. Could Maria prove that what she thought was true? _____

7. How could Bertha help Maria? _____

   _____

   _____

B Skill Item

8. Compare Bertha and a normal 15-year-old girl. Remember, first tell how they're the same. Then tell how they're different.

   _____

   _____

   _____

Review Items

Fill in the blanks on the time line.

9. Write **now** next to the dot that shows the year now.

10. Write **3 thousand years ago** next to the right dot.

11. Write **1 hundred years ago** next to the right dot.

12. Write **2 thousand years ago** next to the right dot.

13. Write **2 hundred years ago** next to the right dot.

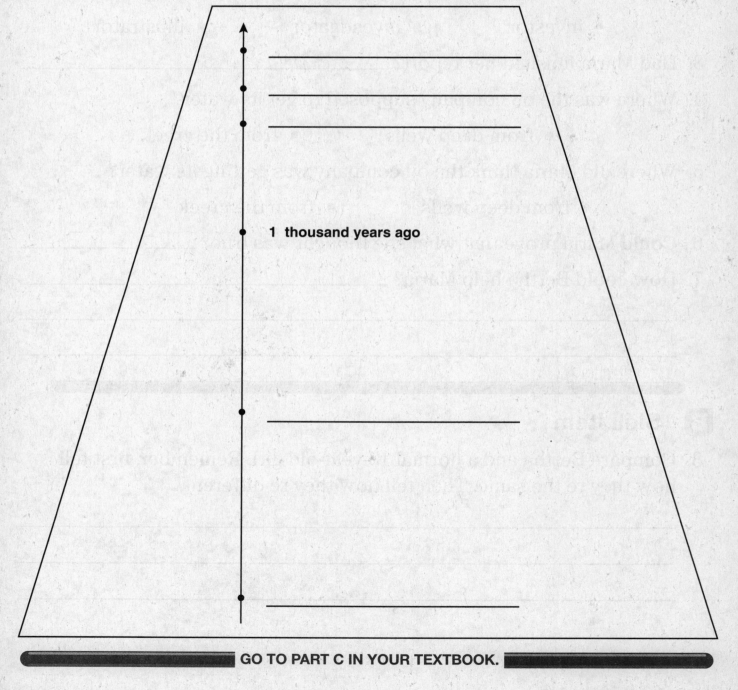

1 thousand years ago

Name _____

1. Name two kinds of wells. _____

Write these names on the picture to show where each liquid is: **crude oil, fresh water, salt water.**

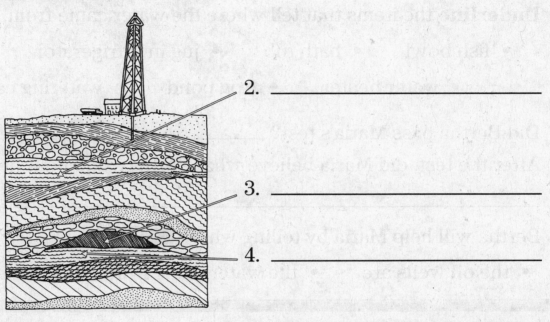

2. _____

3. _____

4. _____

5. Fill in the boxes with the names for the **crude oil, pipeline,** and **refinery.**

6. Draw an arrow at **A** to show which way the crude oil is moving.

7. Draw an arrow at **B** to show which way the crude oil is moving.

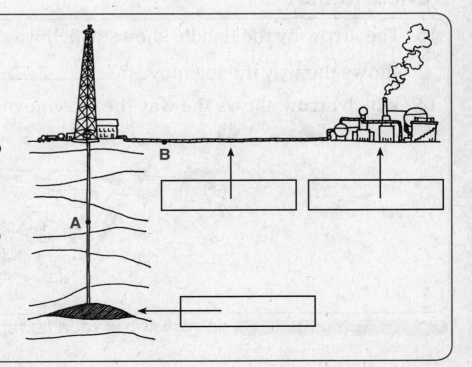

B Story Items

8. Gasoline comes from a liquid called _____.

9. When Bertha first told Maria about her talent, did Maria believe her?

   _____

10. How many glasses of water did Maria use to test Bertha's talent?

    _____

11. **Underline** the items that tell where the water came from.

    - fish bowl   • bath tub   • jug in refrigerator   • sink

        • water heater   • frog pond   • watering can

12. Did Bertha pass Maria's test? _____

13. After the test, did Maria believe what Bertha said about her talent?

    _____

14. Bertha will help Maria by telling where ▬▬▬.

    - the oil wells are   • the water came from   • the snow was

Review Items

15. The arrow by the handle shows which way it turns. Which arrow

    shows the way the log moves? _____

16. Which arrow shows the way the vine moves? _____

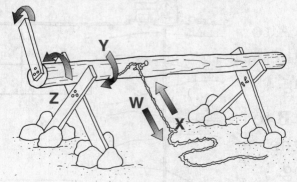

GO TO PART D IN YOUR TEXTBOOK.

Name _____

Story Items

1. What was the name of the oil refinery? _____

2. Name two ways that the oil refinery was like a prison.

   1 _____

   2 _____

3. Was the guard at the gate angry? _____

4. Did he act as if he was angry? _____

5. How did Bertha know that he was angry? _____

6. Name the building that Maria and Bertha drove to.

   _____

7. How many floors did that building have? _____

8. What was on the second floor of the building? _____

9. What was on the third floor of the building? _____

10. Bertha smelled something on the third floor that told her who had

    offices there. What did she smell?

    • lawyers and fish • books • doctors • typists and roast beef

11. What was on the fourth floor of the building? _____

12. How many people did Bertha think worked on the top floor of the

    building? _____

13. Was the author's purpose in this story to **persuade, inform,** or

    entertain? _____

Review Items

14. **Underline** each place that is in the United States.

- Alaska
- New York City
- California
- China
- Japan
- Ohio
- Chicago
- Lake Michigan
- San Francisco
- Turkey
- Italy
- Texas
- Denver

15. When the Greek army put ladders against the wall of Troy, what did the people of Troy do? _____

16. When the Greek army dug holes under the wall, what did the people of Troy do? _____

17. When the Greek army tried to knock down the gate, what did the people of Troy do? _____

18. Why couldn't the Greek army starve the people of Troy? _____

_____

GO TO PART C IN YOUR TEXTBOOK.

Name _____

Story Items

1. On what floor of building C were Maria and Bertha at the beginning of today's story? _____

2. Name two people that Maria and Bertha talked to on the fifth floor.

   _____

3. **Underline** 2 things that were in the first office.

   • huge windows   • a fireplace   • thick walls   • thick rugs

4. Which office was bigger, the office Donna was in or Mr. Daniels' office?

   _____

5. Was Mr. Daniels happy to see Maria? _____

6. Where was Donna going to take Maria and Bertha at the end of the story? _____

   • Building 7   • Building B   • Building 9

7. What were they going to see there? _____

8. Who said that the refinery uses the water in building 9?

   _____

9. Was that person telling the truth?

   _____

Review Items

Write the years where they belong on the time line.

• 1993   • 1998   • 1991   • 1994   • 1996

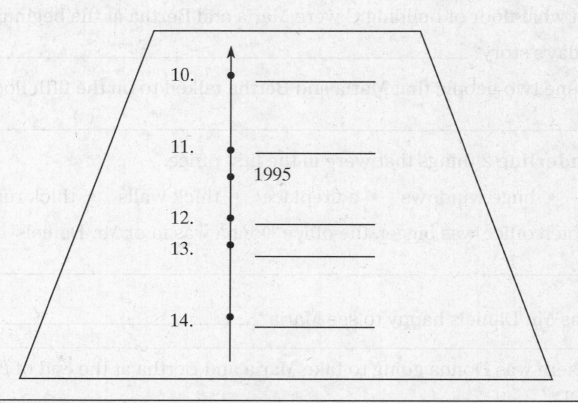

10. _____

11. _____

      1995

12. _____

13. _____

14. _____

Jar M is filled with ocean water. Jar P is filled with fresh water.

15. Which jar is heavier? _____

16. Which jar will freeze at 32 degrees? _____

17. Will the other jar freeze **above 32 degrees**
or **below 32 degrees?**

_____

M   P

GO TO PART D IN YOUR TEXTBOOK.

Name _____

Story Items

1. Did Donna act friendly in this story? _____

2. Bertha's nose told her that Donna felt very ▮▮▮.

     • happy   • uneasy   • scared

3. What kind of building was building 9?

     • an office   • a refinery   • a garage

4. Why did Maria and Bertha go to building 9?

     • to see oil   • to see water   • to see trucks

5. Where did Big Ted say the water came from? _____

6. Was Big Ted telling the truth? _____

7. Did Maria think that the Reef Oil Refinery was trying to trick her?

_____

8. Maria wanted Mr. Daniels to take her to the ▮▮▮.

   • office buildings   • refinery buildings   • garages

9. Did Mr. Daniels want to do that? _____

Review Items

10. Let's say you are outside when the temperature is 50 degrees. What is the temperature inside your body? _____

11. Let's say you are outside when the temperature is 75 degrees. What is the temperature inside your body? _____

12. Let's say a fly is outside when the temperature is 75 degrees. What is the temperature inside the fly's body? _____

13. Would it be easier to catch a fly on a hot day or a cold day?

_____

14. Tell why. _____

_____

15. A plane that flies from Italy to New York City goes in which direction?

_____

16. Where are the fuel tanks on a big jet? _____

17. Write the letter of the plane that is in the warmest air. _____

18. Write the letter of the plane that is in the coldest air. _____

C	5 miles high
B	4 miles high
	3 miles high
D	2 miles high
A	1 mile high

GO TO PART C IN YOUR TEXTBOOK.

Name _____

Story Items

1. Mr. Daniels got Maria in trouble with the chief by telling the chief
    ▮▮▮.

    • lies   • facts   • true stories

2. Maria didn't want the chief to see Bertha when they went to the
    refinery because ▮▮▮.

    • Bertha worked for the state   • Bertha did not work for the state

    • Bertha had an unusual talent

3. Bertha came up with a plan. Where did she hide?

    _____

4. Where did Maria stop the van? _____

5. Who will bring the water near Bertha? _____

6. How will Maria signal that it is all right for Bertha to talk?

    _____

7. What will Bertha tell when Maria gives the signal?

    • Where the van is   • What time it is

    • Where the water came from

8. Maria and Bertha did not practice the plan before they left for the

    refinery because _____.

9. Who was sleepy in the van? _____

10. Why did Bertha start feeling sick? _____

    _____

Review Items

Fill in the blanks on the time line.

11. Write **now** next to the dot that shows the year now.

12. Write **3 thousand years ago** next to the right dot.

13. Write **1 thousand years ago** next to the right dot.

14. Write **1 hundred years ago** next to the right dot.

15. Write **2 hundred years ago** next to the right dot.

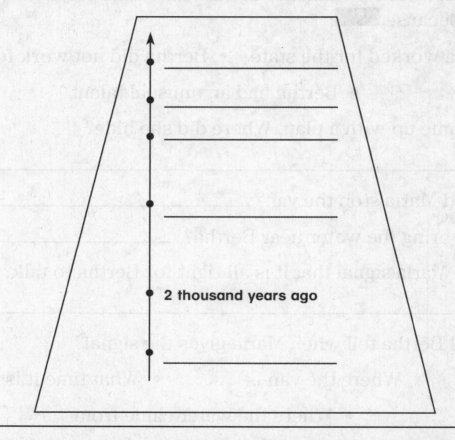

2 thousand years ago

16. During the war with Troy, what did the Greek army build to help them get inside Troy? _____

17. What was inside this object? _____

18. What did they do after they came out of the object?

_____

19. Who won the war, Troy or Greece? _____

GO TO PART C IN YOUR TEXTBOOK.

Name _____

Story Items

1. What happened to the crude oil in building twenty-one?

    • It became gasoline.   • It became darker.

    • It became water.

2. There was a very strong smell at building twenty-one. What was that

    smell? _____

3. The inside of the van kept getting _____.

4. When Bertha smelled the water that the refinery was using, she knew

    where the water was from. Where was it from? _____

5. Why did Bertha faint? _____

6. Make a **T** on the shadow of the tree.

7. Make a **C** on the shadow of the car.

8. Make an **H** on the shadow of the house.

Review Items

9. Why didn't the people of Troy have cars?

    - There were no cars yet.   • Cars cost too much.

                • They liked horses better.

10. The people of Troy got in and out of the city through the great

    _____.

11. How many ships sailed to Troy? _____

12. How long did the war between Greece and Troy go on?

    _____.

13. If the Greek army could get a few men inside the wall of Troy, those

    men could _____.

14. Name 2 kinds of wells. _____

15. Gasoline comes from a liquid called _____.

GO TO PART C IN YOUR TEXTBOOK.

Name _____

Story Items

1. **Underline** 2 things that Bertha told about the chief to prove her talent.

   - He lived north of town.   • He had 3 dogs.
   - He had a dog.   • He lived near cottonwood trees.

2. How did Mr. Daniels act while the chief was asking Bertha questions?

   • angry   • nice   • quiet

3. What did Bertha tell the chief about the water that the refinery was

   using? _____

4. The water had something in it that let Bertha know where the water

   was from. What was in the water? _____

5. At the end of the story, the chief told Maria to get six jars of water.

   How many will come from the well? _____

6. How many will come from the creek? _____

7. What do you think the chief will do with the water?

   _____

Review Items

8. How many legs does an insect have? _____

9. How many legs does a fly have? _____

10. How many legs does a bee have? _____

11. How many legs does a spider have? _____

12. How many parts does a spider's body have? _____

13. How many parts does a fly's body have? _____

14. How far is it from New York City to San Francisco?

_____

15. How far is it from San Francisco to Japan?

_____

16. What ocean do you cross to get from San Francisco to Japan?

_____

Skill Item

17. Compare creek water and well water. Remember what you're going to tell first and what you're going to tell next.

_____

_____

_____

GO TO PART C IN YOUR TEXTBOOK.

Name _____

Story Items

1. How many blindfolds did Bertha have on when she tested the water?

   _____

2. **Underline** each blindfold.

   - a blue mask
   - a long cloth
   - tape
   - dark glasses
   - a leather belt
   - a hood

3. The chief put blindfolds on Bertha so she couldn't _____

   _____.

4. When Bertha tested the water, the chief didn't let her touch the jars of water so she wouldn't know the ▮▮▮.

   - temperature
   - weight
   - color

5. How many jars of water did Bertha test? _____

6. How many jars did she get wrong? _____

7. How did Mr. Daniels act after the test? _____

8. The chief ordered Mr. Daniels to ▮▮▮ the refinery.

   - sell
   - buy
   - close

9. When was Mr. Daniels to do that?

   - immediately
   - within a month
   - within a year

10. The chief wanted Bertha to be ▮▮▮.

    - a teacher
    - a special consultant
    - a driver

11. How much will Bertha earn each day? _____

Lesson 78   **51**

Review Items

12. What do all living things need? _____

13. What do all living things make? _____

14. Do all living things grow? _____

15. Are flies living things? _____

16. **Underline** 3 things you know about flies.

- Flies make babies.
- Flies grow.
- Flies need water.
- Flies need ants.
- Flies need sugar.

17. Some of the lines in the box are one inch long and some are one centimeter long. Write the letter of every line that is one centimeter long. _____

18. Write the letter of every line that is one inch long. _____

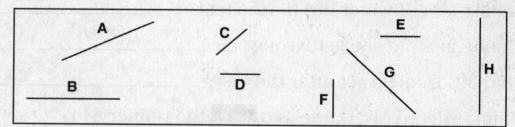

GO TO PART C IN YOUR TEXTBOOK.

A

FORM 50:
SPECIAL CONSULTANTS AND GROUP LEADERS

1. Have you been paid to work for the state before? _____

2. How old are you? _____

3. Print your full name. _____

4. Do you want to be a **special consultant** or a **group leader?**

   _____

5. Do you have your own car? _____

6. How much will you earn every day? _____

7. What is your special talent? _____

If you are to be a group leader, answer these questions:

8. How many are in your group? _____

9. What is your special topic? _____

If you are to be a special consultant, answer this question:

10. What's the name of the investigator you work with?

    _____

B Story Items

11. Where did Achilles' mother take him when he was a baby?

    _____

12. Why did she want to dip him in the river?

    - to clean him
    - to make sure nothing could harm him
    - to teach him to swim

13. **Finish the rule about the water in the river.** If the water touched a part of your body, _____.

14. If you put your arm in the magic river, what would happen to your arm? _____

15. Achilles' mother held on to part of him when she dipped him in the river. What part? _____

16. What part of Achilles did not get wet? _____

17. What part of Achilles could get hurt? _____

18. Achilles was in the army from ▮▮▮▮.

    • Italy   • Greece   • Troy

19. Why were all the soldiers afraid of Achilles?

    _____

20. Is the story about Achilles a true story? _____

GO TO PART D IN YOUR TEXTBOOK.

Name _____

Story Items

1. How many ships went to war with Troy? _____

2. Which army was Achilles in? _____

3. How long was Achilles in the war? _____

4. Who was the greatest soldier of Troy? _____

5. Who won when Achilles and Hector fought? _____

6. Achilles rode around the wall of Troy in a _____.

7. How did the people of Troy feel when Achilles killed Hector?

   _____

8. Did the arrows that hit Achilles in the chest hurt him? _____

9. The arrow that killed Achilles hit him in the _____.

10. The arrow had something on it that killed Achilles. What did it have on it?

    • powder   • poison   • paint

Review Items

11. The temperature inside your body is about _____ degrees when you are healthy.

12. Most fevers don't go over _____ degrees.

13. The place that is called Troy is now part of what country?

    • Greece   • Turkey   • Italy

Review Items

Here are the facts you need to fill out the form below: Your name is Sam Lee and you want to work as a group leader. You are 22 years old and you have your own car. You have worked for the state before and you will earn $300 per day. Your special topic is "Safe Driving." There are 50 people in your group.

FORM 50

SPECIAL CONSULTANTS AND GROUP LEADERS

14. Print your full name. _____

15. How old are you? _____

16. Have you worked for the state before? _____

17. Do you have your own car? _____

18. How much will you earn every day? _____

19. Do you want to be a **special consultant** or a **group leader?**

    _____

If you are to be a group leader, answer these questions:

20. How many are in your group? _____

21. What is your special topic? _____

If you are to be a special consultant, answer this question:

22. What's the name of the investigator you work with?

    _____

GO TO PART D IN YOUR TEXTBOOK.

Name _____

Story Items

1. People who lived 80 thousand years ago did not have many things that we have today. **Underline** 4 things they did not have.

   - TV sets   • bones   • phones   • refrigerators
   - food   • rocks   • dogs   • books

2. What clue could tell you that someone ate chicken? _____
   _____

3. What clue could tell you that someone ate a coconut? _____

4. What's a good place to look for clues about people who lived long
   ago? _____

5. Some people who lived 80 thousand years ago lived in _____.

6. Name 2 clues that tell us that dogs may have lived with people 8
   thousand years ago. _____
   _____

7. Name one clue that tells us how people may have hunted large
   animals like buffalo. _____
   _____

8. Name 2 clues that tell us that people used fire to cook their food.
   _____

9. Did the first people who lived in caves cook their food? _____

10. Did the people who lived in caves many years later cook their food?
    _____

11. Was the author's purpose to **persuade, inform,** or **entertain?**
    _____

Review Items

Here's how fast different things can go:

- 200 miles per hour
- 20 miles per hour
- 500 miles per hour
- 35 miles per hour

12. Which speed tells how fast a fast dog can run? _____

13. Which speed tells how fast a jet can fly? _____

14. Which speed tells how fast a fast man can run? _____

15. Which army was Achilles in during the war between Troy and Greece? _____

16. How long was Achilles in the war? _____

17. Who was the greatest soldier of Troy? _____

18. Who won when Hector and Achilles fought? _____

19. Achilles rode around the wall of Troy in a _____.

20. The arrow that killed Achilles hit him in the _____.

21. That arrow had something on it that killed Achilles. What did it have on it? _____

GO TO PART C IN YOUR TEXTBOOK.

Name _____

1. Things closer to the bottom of the pile went into the pile _____.

2. Things closer to the top of the pile went into the pile _____.

The picture below shows a pile of garbage.

3. Write the words **earlier** and **later** in the right boxes.

4. Which thing went into the pile earlier, thing M or thing B? _____

5. Which thing went into the pile earlier, thing A or thing S? _____

6. Which thing went into the pile later, thing A or thing B? _____

7. Which thing went into the pile later, thing M or thing R? _____

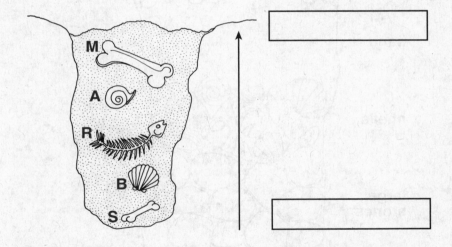

8. What clues would tell us that people used fire to cook their food?

_____

9. Did the first people who lived in caves cook their food? _____

10. How do we know? _____

Lesson 83 **59**

The picture below shows a hole dug near a beach.

11. When we dig into the pile, what's the first thing we find?

_____

12. What's the next thing we find? _____

13. What's the next thing we find? _____

14. What's the next thing we find? _____

15. What's the last thing we find? _____

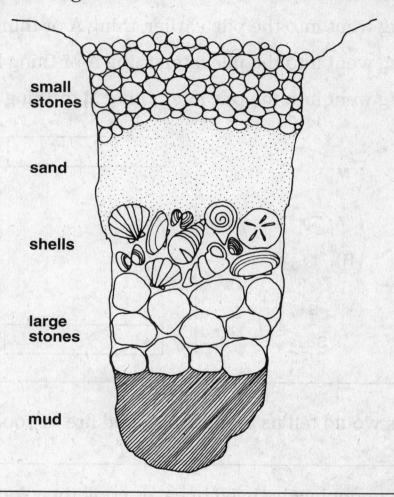

small stones

sand

shells

large stones

mud

GO TO PART C IN YOUR TEXTBOOK.

Name _____

A

1. Which picture shows how you should hold a burning branch if you don't want to get burned? _____

2. Draw an arrow from each dot to show which way the heat will move.

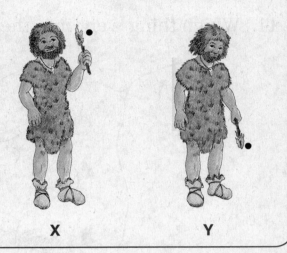

X   Y

3. How does fire like to move, up or down? _____

B Story Items

4. Write **north, south, east,** and **west** in the right boxes.

5. The wind blows from the north. Draw an arrow from the dot to show that wind.

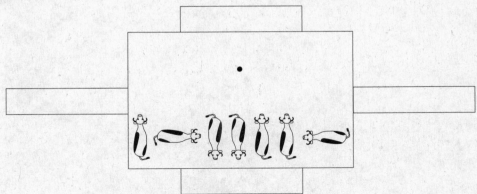

6. **Circle** every cow that is facing north.

Review Items

7. Write the words **earlier** and **later** in the right boxes.

8. Which thing went into the pile earlier, thing M or thing A? _____

9. Which thing went into the pile earlier, thing B or thing R? _____

10. Which thing went into the pile later, thing S or thing B? _____

11. Which thing went into the pile later, thing A or thing R? _____

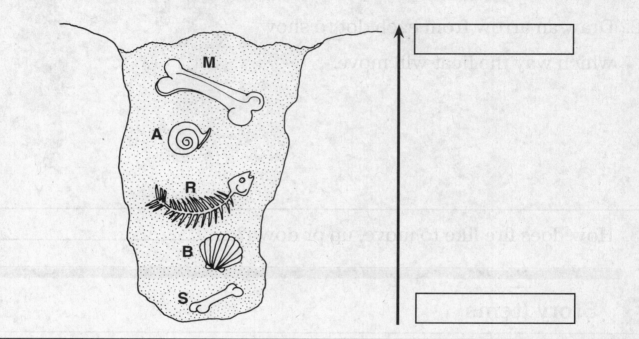

GO TO PART D IN YOUR TEXTBOOK.

Name _____

1. The people who lived in caves drew pictures on the cave walls.
   Underline 3 things they made pictures of.

   • cows   • fish   • birds   • hands   • horses

2. Hand A is the hand of .   • a child   • an adult   • an ape

3. Name one thing you can tell about hand B.

   _____

4. Name 2 ways that hand A is different from hand C.

   _____

   _____

   A   B   C

5. **Underline** 3 things that cave people used to make paint.

   • fat   • hair   • earth   • salt   • blood

The picture shows the outline of a hand on a cave wall.

6. Make an **X** on the part of the wall that was covered
   with paint.

7. Make a **Y** on the part of the wall that was not
   covered with paint.

8. Cave people painted pictures of horses on cave walls. How are those
   horses different from horses that live today?

   _____

9. Some kinds of animals that lived thousands of years ago are not alive today. We know what those animals looked like because we have found ▪▪▪▪.

- hair
- bones
- living animals

Review Items

Fill in the blanks on the time line.

10. Write **now** next to the dot that shows the year now.

11. Write **3 thousand years ago** next to the right dot.

12. Write **1 thousand years ago** next to the right dot.

13. Write **1 hundred years ago** next to the right dot.

14. Write **2 thousand years ago** next to the right dot.

2 hundred years ago

GO TO PART C IN YOUR TEXTBOOK.

Name _____

Under each horse, write what kind of horse is shown.

• Mongolian horse   • racehorse   • pony   • draft horse   • quarter horse

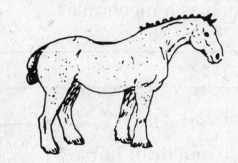

1. _____   2. _____

3. _____   4. _____   5. _____

6. What 3 things are quarter horses good at doing?

   • turning   • running fast   • stopping

      • starting fast   • pulling heavy loads

7. How many third-graders weigh as much as a quarter horse?

   _____

8. What are draft horses good at doing?

   • turning   • running fast   • stopping

      • starting fast   • pulling heavy loads

9. How many third-graders weigh as much as a draft horse? _____

10. The Mongolian horse was the kind of horse that lived _____
    thousand years ago.

11. How many third-graders weigh as much as a Mongolian horse?

_____

12. What are racehorses good at doing? _____

13. How tall is a racehorse at the head? _____

14. How many third-graders weigh as much as a racehorse?

_____

15. How tall is a pony at the shoulder? _____

16. How many third-graders weigh as much as a pony? _____

17. Which horse has thin legs, a racehorse or a draft horse?

_____

18. Which horse has a shorter back, a racehorse or a quarter horse?

_____

Review Items

19. A speedometer tells about ▮▮▮▮ .

    • hours   • miles per hour   • miles

20. The people who lived in caves drew pictures on the cave walls. Write
    the letters of 4 things they made pictures of. _____

    a. hands   b. fish   c. bears   d. dogs

    e. horses   f. cows   g. birds   h. elephants

21. Cave people painted pictures of horses on cave walls. How are those
    horses different from horses that live today?

    _____

GO TO PART C IN YOUR TEXTBOOK.

Name _____

Story Items

1. Write the words **earlier** and **later** in the right boxes.

2. How many years ago did layer A go into the pile?

_____

3. How many years ago did layer B go into the pile?

_____

4. How many years ago did layer C go into the pile?

_____

5. How many years ago did layer D go into the pile?

_____

6. How many years ago did layer E go into the pile?

_____

E — NOW
Story of Troy
30 thousand years ago

D — 1 million years ago

C — 11 million years ago

B — 28 million years ago

A — 38 million years ago

7. The horse skeleton in layer A is no bigger than a ▮▮▮▮.

　　　• small dog　　• pony　　• big dog

8. The horse skeleton in layer B is about as big as a ▮▮▮▮.

　　　• small dog　　• pony　　• big dog

9. The horse skeleton in layer C is about as big as a ▮▮▮▮.

　　　• small dog　　• pony　　• big dog

10. The people who lived in caves drew pictures on the cave walls. **Underline** 4 things they made pictures of.

• hands • feet • cats • elephants • horses • dogs • birds • cows

11. Things closer to the bottom of the pile

_____.

12. Things closer to the top of the pile

_____.

13. How was the earliest horse different from horses that live today?

_____

14. The earliest horses on Earth are not alive today. How long ago did the earliest horses live?

• 38 thousand years ago   • 28 years ago

• 38 million years ago   • 30 thousand years ago

Review Items

Write what kind of horse each picture shows.

• racehorse • quarter horse • pony • Mongolian horse • draft horse

15. _____ 16. _____ 17. _____

18. _____ 19. _____

GO TO PART C IN YOUR TEXTBOOK.

Name _____

Story Items

1. Eohippus lived _____ million years ago.

2. **Underline** 2 ways that the front legs of eohippus were different from the front legs of a horse that lives today.

   - They were smaller.   • They had smaller hooves.

   - They didn't have hooves.   • They were faster.

3. The changes in the legs made horses _____.

4. Who was faster, eohippus or large cats? _____

5. Over millions of years, what happened to the size of horses?

   _____

6. Bigger animals are safer because ▮▮▮.

   - not as many animals run faster

   - not as many animals are smaller

   - not as many animals hunt bigger animals

7. Which animal is safer, an elephant or a mouse? _____

8. Tell why. _____

9. Was the author's purpose to **persuade, inform,** or **entertain?**

   _____

Review Items

10. The horse skeleton in layer A is no bigger than a ▮▮▮.

    • big dog   • small dog   • pony

11. The horse skeleton in layer B is about as big as a ▮▮▮.

    • big dog   • small dog   • pony

12. The horse skeleton in layer C is about as big as a ▮▮▮.

    • big dog   • small dog   • pony

13. Write the words **earlier** and **later** in the right boxes.

14. How many years ago did layer A go into the pile?

    _____

15. How many years ago did layer B go into the pile?

    _____

16. How many years ago did layer C go into the pile?

    _____

17. How many years ago did layer D go into the pile?

    _____

18. How many years ago did layer E go into the pile?

    _____

E   NOW
     Story of Troy
     30 thousand
     years ago

D   1 million
     years ago

C   11 million
     years ago

B   28 million
     years ago

A   38 million
     years ago

GO TO PART C IN YOUR TEXTBOOK.

Name _____

A

Pretend you are Bertha and fill out the form below. The facts that you need are in Part B on page 307 of your textbook.

1. Last Name _____ 2. First Name _____

3. Street Address _____

4. City _____ 5. State _____

6. Phone Number _____

7. How much money are you putting in the bank? $ _____

B **Story Items**

8. What do people keep in banks? _____

9. What kind of job did Andrew Dexter have? _____

10. When Andrew was young, was he very strong? _____

11. In high school, Andrew went out for 3 teams. **Underline** those 3 teams.

• soccer   • basketball   • hockey   • baseball   • golf   • tennis   • football

12. Was Andrew good enough for the teams? _____

13. Andrew spent lots of time doing 2 things. Name those 2 things.

_____

14. In real life, did many people love Andrew? _____

15. In Andrew's dreams, how did people feel about him?

_____

16. What kind of place is in this picture? _____

17. **Circle** the teller.

18. Write **C** on the counter.

19. Write **P** on the person who is giving money to the teller.

20. Write **L** on the person who is leaving.

GO TO PART D IN YOUR TEXTBOOK.

Name _____

A

1. When was the check below written? _____

2. Who should the bank pay? _____

3. How much should the bank pay? _____

4. Whose money should the bank use to pay Tom Lee?

_____

March 10, 2006

Pay to _____Tom Lee_____ $10

_____Ten_____ **dollars**

Rod Mack

B Story Items

5. When Andrew said, "Thank you" to the first customer, what did the

first customer say? _____

6. When the second customer came to Andrew, Andrew was
daydreaming. What was he daydreaming about?

- football   • baseball   • basketball

7. Andrew noticed something on the counter when he finished with the second customer. What was on the counter? _____

8. Where did Mr. Franks want Andrew to take the package?
   - to Magnetic Research Company   • to Magnetic Tape Company
                    • to Magnetic Refill Company

9. Did Andrew know what was in the package? _____

10. Was the package **heavy** or **light?** _____

11. As Andrew drove to Magnetic Research Company, what was he thinking about? _____

12. Why did a woman in a car yell at Andrew?

    _____

13. After the woman yelled at him, he told himself to pay attention to

    _____.

GO TO PART D IN YOUR TEXTBOOK.

Name _____

Story Items

1. Name 2 things that a strong magnet can pick up.

   _____

2. Electricity can turn any steel bar into a magnet. What are these

   magnets called? _____

3. **Underline** a place where these magnets are used.

   • schools   • wrecking yards   • parks   • banks

4. Andrew walked into a room that was filled with something. What
   was it filled with?

   • garbage   • fish   • electricity

5. What made the motor in the package run? _____

6. Magnetic Research Company planned to put this kind of motor in .

   • toasters   • refrigerators   • parks   • cars

7. When Andrew walked into the room, the motor melted and burned

   Andrew's _____.

8. Did Andrew know what had happened to him? _____

9. How did Andrew's legs and arms feel when he left Magnetic Research

   Company? _____

10. What happened when Andrew tugged at his car door? _____

    _____

Review Items

Fill out the bank form below using these facts.

- Your name is Sally Andrews.

- You're going to put $100 in the bank.

- You live at 144 High Street, Redding, California.

- Your phone number is 555-3434.

11. Last name _____ 12. First name _____

13. Phone number _____

14. Street address _____

15. City _____ 16. State _____

17. How much money are you putting in the bank? _____

18. What do people keep in banks? _____

19. Roots keep a tree from _____.

20. Roots carry _____ to all parts of the tree.

21. In which season is the danger of forest fires greatest? _____

22. **Underline** the 4 names that tell about time.

- week   • inch   • centimeter   • second

- minute   • meter   • hour

23. A mile is a little more than ▮▮▮ feet.

- 1 thousand   • 5 thousand   • 5 hundred

GO TO PART C IN YOUR TEXTBOOK.

A

1. About how much does a leopard weigh?

    • 100 pounds   • 150 pounds   • 500 pounds

2. About how much weight can a leopard carry? _____

3. About how much does a chimpanzee weigh? _____

4. About how much force can a chimpanzee pull with? _____

B **Story Items**

5. Andrew is now as strong as ▮▮▮▮.

    • an alligator   • an African elephant   • a leopard

6. Andrew knew that Mr. Franks was mad by looking at his

    _____.

7. Andrew didn't ring the bell by the front door at Magnetic Research
   Company. Tell why.

    _____

8. What happened to Andrew after Mr. Franks had a talk with him?

    • Andrew was fried.   • Andrew was tired.   • Andrew was fired.

9. How high did Andrew jump to catch the baseball? _____

10. Had anybody ever jumped that high before Andrew did? _____

11. Andrew threw the ball to the catcher. How fast did that ball move?

    _____

The catcher is going to catch three different balls. Look at the speed of the three baseballs flying through the air. One ball will knock the catcher over. One ball will knock the catcher back a little bit, but it won't knock him over. One ball will do nothing.

12. Write **knock over** next to the ball that will knock the catcher over.

13. Start at the dot and make an arrow under the catcher to show which way he will fall when the ball knocks him over.

14. Write **knock a little** next to the ball that will knock the catcher back a little.

15. Write **nothing** next to the ball that will not knock the catcher back at all.

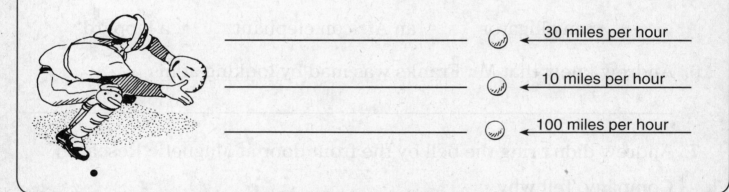

30 miles per hour

10 miles per hour

100 miles per hour

GO TO PART D IN YOUR TEXTBOOK.

Name _____

A

> **Write the name of each part of a football player's uniform.**
>
> • shoulders • hat • shoulder pads • knee pads • helmet
>
>
>
> 1. _____ 2. _____

3. How long is a football field? _____

4. **Underline** 2 ways that a football team can move the ball down the field.

    • slide   • pass   • roll   • run

5. If a team moves the ball all the way to the other end of the field, that team gets points. How many points? _____

6. If team A has the ball, team B tries to ▬▬▬.

    • kick the ball   • catch the passes

    • tackle the player with the ball   • kick the player with the ball

B **Story Items**

7. Andrew did two impossible things at the playground. How high did he jump? _____

8. How fast did he throw the ball? _____

9. Denny Brock was a ▬▬▬.

    • player   • guard   • coach

Lesson 94   **79**

10. Denny Brock was almost always mad because his team was

_____.

11. The people who owned the Titans were unhappy. Who did they say
they might fire? _____

12. How many fans came to the ball park to watch most professional
teams? _____

13. How many fans came to the ball park to watch the Titans?

_____

14. Why did Andrew lie to the guard? _____

_____

15. Did Denny want to talk to Andrew? _____

16. What did Denny say he would do if Andrew didn't leave?

_____

Skill Items

Here's the rule: **The more fans that come to a game, the more money the team gets from tickets.**

17. **Circle** the name of the team that gets the most money from tickets.

18. **Underline** the name of the team that gets the least money from tickets.

- Rams .... 50 thousand fans
- Wildcats .... 60 thousand fans
- Jets .... 40 thousand fans
- Chargers .... 50 thousand fans
- Spartans .... 30 thousand fans
- Bulls .... 50 thousand fans

GO TO PART D IN YOUR TEXTBOOK.

A

1. A second is a unit of ▉▉▉.

  • weight   • length   • time

2. Which stopwatch shows that 2 seconds have passed? _____

3. Which stopwatch shows that 6 seconds have passed? _____

4. Which stopwatch shows that 8 seconds have passed? _____

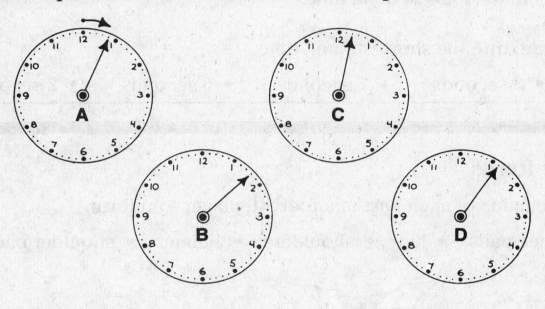

B **Story Items**

5. The player who pulled his leg muscle was the ▉▉▉ for the Titans.

  • passer   • kicker   • runner

6. How did Denny feel about that player getting hurt? _____

7. Did Denny believe that Andrew could kick? _____

8. Did Andrew know what hang-time is? _____

9. Andrew didn't tell what hang-time is because he was ▉▉▉.

  • uneasy   • sweating   • smiling

Lesson 95 **81**

10. If the hang-time for a kick is 4 seconds, how long does the ball stay in the air? _____

11. Andrew was standing on the field holding the football. Who was watching him? _____

12. Denny told Andrew, "I want to see a _____-second hang-time."

13. **Circle** the longest hang-time.

14. **Underline** the shortest hang-time.

- 3 seconds   • 7 seconds   • 5 seconds   • 2 seconds

Review Items

Write the name of each part of a football player's uniform.

- knee pads • hat • shoulders • helmet • shoulder pads

15. _____   16. _____

GO TO PART D IN YOUR TEXTBOOK.

Name _____

Story Items

1. Andrew kicked the football two times. Why was it hard to see the ball when Andrew kicked it?

   - It moved so fast.   • It moved so slowly.
   - It made so much noise.

2. The coaches and players were silent right after Andrew kicked the ball the first time because they were ▮▮▮▮.

   - watching Andrew   • watching the ball   • making jokes

3. When the first ball stopped rolling, the players began to yell at Andrew. What did they want Andrew to do? _____

4. What was Andrew's hang-time the first time he kicked the ball?

   _____

5. What was Andrew's hang-time the second time he kicked the ball?

   _____

6. How many people in the world besides Andrew could kick a ball with a hang-time of more than 9 seconds? _____

7. After his second kick how did the players treat Andrew?

   _____

8. Denny was being nice to Andrew at the end of the story because he wanted Andrew to _____.

9. Was the author's purpose to **persuade, inform** or **entertain?**

   _____.

Review Items

10. Did the first people who lived in caves cook their food? _____

11. Did the people who lived in caves many years later cook their food?

    _____

12. The picture shows the outline of a hand on a cave wall. Which letter shows the part of the wall that was covered with paint? _____

13. Which letter shows the part of the wall that was not covered with paint? _____

GO TO PART C IN YOUR TEXTBOOK.

Name _____

1. Who makes more money, a professional football player or a bank teller?

_____

2. Which football players are worth the most money?

- the worst players

- the players that fans want to see

- the fastest players

3. A football player who is very good at running with the ball may

earn 3 _____ a year.

B Story Items

4. When Andrew said that he would play for the Titans, Denny didn't jump up and down with joy. What did Denny think Andrew was trying to do?

- be friendly   • work hard   • trick him

5. When Denny wants a player for the Titans, he makes an offer to the

player. Does the player usually take that offer? _____

6. So Denny makes a new offer. For this offer Denny offers ▮▮▮.

- less money   • the same money   • more money

7. Denny knew that if Andrew was on the team, fans would come to the games even if the Titans lost. Why would they come?

_____

8. How much was Andrew worth for each game that he played?

- more than 1 million dollars
- less than 1 million dollars
- 200 thousand dollars
- 2 hundred dollars each month
- 2 thousand dollars each month
- 20 thousand dollars each month

9. How much money did Andrew ask for?

_____

10. How much money per month did Denny say he would pay Andrew?

_____

11. How much money is that per year?

- 100 thousand dollars   • 240 dollars   • 240 thousand dollars

12. After the men shook hands, both men were happy. Denny was happy because he _____

_____.

13. Andrew was happy because he _____

_____.

Review Items

14. What part of a car tells how fast the car is moving?

_____

15. Which army was Achilles in during the war between Troy and Greece? _____

16. How long was Achilles in the war? _____

17. Who was the greatest soldier of Troy? _____

18. Who won when Hector and Achilles fought? _____

19. Achilles rode around the wall of Troy in a _____

GO TO PART D IN YOUR TEXTBOOK.

Name _____

Story Items

1. Before Andrew's first game, announcements appeared in the newspapers. The announcements gave the impression that Andrew could turn the Titans into ▮▮▮▮.

    • a baseball team   • a winning team   • a losing team

2. Did the announcements tell what Andrew could do? _____

3. How many fans came to Andrew's first game?

    _____

4. Who were the fans talking about?

    _____

5. The fans didn't think the Titans would win because they were playing

    _____.

6. How did the players feel just before the game started?

    • sleepy   • nervous   • happy

7. Andrew was more frightened than the other players because he had never ▮▮▮▮.

    • seen 50 thousand people   • played in front of 50 thousand people

8. Who kicked the ball at the beginning of the game? _____

9. Which team caught the ball? _____

10. How far was the ball from the goal line? _____

11. How far did the Titans need to go to score their first touchdown?

    _____

12. The Wildcats got the ball. Tell **2** ways they moved the ball down the field. _____

13. How did the Titans get the ball back?
   • A Wildcat passed the ball.   • A Wildcat fumbled the ball.
                        • A Wildcat ran with the ball.

14. What did the crowd do when the Titans began to lose yards?

    _____

15. Did the crowd laugh when they heard that Andrew was going to kick an 80-yard goal? _____

GO TO PART C IN YOUR TEXTBOOK.

Name _____

Story Items

1. How far did Andrew kick the ball?

    • 100 yards   • 200 yards   • 180 yards

2. It wasn't a field goal because it didn't _____

    _____.

3. The Wildcats were winning, and the Titans were getting hurt. Name the player who was hurting the Titans. _____

4. **Underline** 3 things that tell what Smiling Sam looked like.

    • small   had no hair   • had a friendly smile   • old
    • fast   • had missing teeth   • had a mean smile   • big

5. The coach didn't want Andrew to talk to Smiling Sam because he thought _____.

6. Andrew talked to Smiling Sam anyway. Did Andrew scare Smiling Sam? _____

7. When the ball came to Andrew, he waited for somebody. Who?

    _____

8. **Underline** 3 things that happened to Smiling Sam when Andrew hit him.

    • Sam tackled Andrew.   • Sam was knocked out.

              • Sam's teeth were loose.

    • Sam's shirt was torn.   • Sam flew backwards.

9. Why were the Titans surprised when Andrew ran with the ball?

_____

10. In the game with the Wildcats, Andrew scored _____ touchdowns.

11. Which team won the game? _____

Review Items

Fill out the bank form below using these facts.

- Your name is Zack Morris.

- You're going to put $50 in the bank.

- You live at 1252 Main Street, Fort Worth, Texas.

- Your phone number is 651-1222.

12. Last name _____ 13. First name _____

14. Phone number _____

15. Street address _____

16. City _____ 17. State _____

18. How much money are you putting in the bank? _____

GO TO PART C IN YOUR TEXTBOOK.

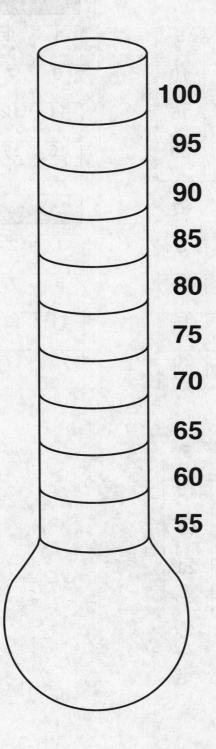

100

95

90

85

80

75

70

65

60

55

Fact Game Scorecards

Lesson 60

1	2	3	4	5
6	7	8	9	10
11	12	13	14	15
16	17	18	19	20

Lesson 90

1	2	3	4	5
6	7	8	9	10
11	12	13	14	15
16	17	18	19	20

Lesson 70

1	2	3	4	5
6	7	8	9	10
11	12	13	14	15
16	17	18	19	20

Lesson 100

1	2	3	4	5
6	7	8	9	10
11	12	13	14	15
16	17	18	19	20

Lesson 80

1	2	3	4	5
6	7	8	9	10
11	12	13	14	15
16	17	18	19	20